3                                         599.83 THR

# LEARNING.
## services

01209 722146

## Duchy College Rosewarne
*Learning Centre*

This resource is to be returned on or before the last date
stamped below. To renew items please contact the Centre

## Three Week Loan

| - 5 NOV 2014 | | |
|---|---|---|
| | | |
| | | |
| | | |

# LIVING IN THE WILD: PRIMATES

# LEMURS

Claire Throp

**www.raintreepublishers.co.uk**
Visit our website to find out more information about Raintree books.

**To order:**
☎ Phone 0845 6044371
▤ Fax +44 (0) 1865 312263
🖳 Email myorders@raintreepublishers.co.uk

Customers from outside the UK please telephone +44 1865 312262

Raintree is an imprint of Capstone Global Library Limited, a company incorporated in England and Wales having its registered office at 7 Pilgrim Street, London, EC4V 6LB – Registered company number: 6695582

Text © Capstone Global Library Limited 2012
First published in hardback in 2012
The moral rights of the proprietor have been asserted.

Edited by Abby Colich, Jilly Hunt, and Vaarunika Dharmapala
Designed by Victoria Allen
Picture research by Tracy Cummins
Original illustrations © Capstone Global Library Ltd 2012
Illustrations by Oxford Designers & Illustrators and HL Studios
Originated by Capstone Global Library Ltd
Printed and bound in China by CTPS

ISBN 978 1 406 23304 9 (hardback)
16 15 14 13 12
10 9 8 7 6 5 4 3 2 1

**British Library Cataloguing in Publication Data**
Throp, Claire.
Lemurs. -- (Living in the wild. Primates)
599.8'3-dc22
A full catalogue record for this book is available from the British Library.

**Acknowledgements**
We would like to thank the following for permission to reproduce photographs: Animals Animals – Earth Scenes p. 33 (© Ardea/M. Watson); Alamy pp. 37 (© Elizabeth Leyden), 40 (© A&J Visage); FLPA pp. 23 (Cyril Ruoso/Minden Pictures), 24 (Chris & Tilde Stuart), 27 (GTW/Imagebroker), 38 (Cyril Ruoso/Minden Pictures), 44 (Silvestris Fotoservice); Getty Images p. 35 (Martin Harvey); istockphoto p. 19 (© Harkamal Nijjar); Photolibrary pp. 7 (Michael Sewell), 11 (jspix jspix), 13 (Nigel Pavitt), 15 (Nick Garbutt), 25 (Martin Harvey), 29 (David Haring), 31 (Cyril Ruoso), 32 (David Haring), 36 (Frans Lemmens), 41 (jspix jspix), 42 (Creativ Studio Heinemann); Photoshot pp. 9 (Nick Garbutt/NHPA), 30 (Kevin Schafer); Shutterstock pp. 5 (© cameilia), 12 (© Hugh Lansdown), 14 (© Ivan Kuzmin), 17 (© Animal), 21 (© David Thyberg); Visuals Unlimited, Inc. p. 16 (Joe McDonald).

Cover photograph of a Verreaux's sifaka in Madagascar, Africa, reproduced with permission of Photolibrary (Bruno De Faveri).

Every effort has been made to contact copyright holders of any material reproduced in this book. Any omissions will be rectified in subsequent printings if notice is given to the publisher.

**Disclaimer**
All the internet addresses (URLs) given in this book were valid at the time of going to press. However, due to the dynamic nature of the internet, some addresses may have changed, or sites may have changed or ceased to exist since publication. While the author and publisher regret any inconvenience this may cause readers, no responsibility for any such changes can be accepted by either the author or the publisher.

# Contents

Some words are shown in bold, **like this**. You can find out what they mean by looking in the glossary.

# What are primates?

What was that? Something moved in the trees! It was a woolly lemur leaping from tree to tree. Lemurs use their powerful legs to push themselves a distance of up to 10 metres (33 feet).

There are thought to be more than 350 **species** of primates. These include lemurs, apes, monkeys – and humans! Our closest relatives are apes and monkeys. We are very alike in many ways. Primates are **mammals**. This means they have hair or fur on their bodies and produce milk for their babies to drink.

This map shows where in the world non-human primates live.

NORTH AMERICA

*Atlantic Ocean*

EUROPE

ASIA

AFRICA

*Pacific Ocean*

*Pacific Ocean*

SOUTH AMERICA

*Indian Ocean*

AUSTRALASIA

Key

Non-human primate habitats

ANTARCTICA

## Common features

Primates can be very different but they also have many things in common. Primates are mainly arboreal, which means they live in trees. They are also intelligent. They can think about problems and try to solve them. They can learn new skills and pass them on to their young. The other thing they share is a desire to be social, which means they like to live with others. Many species of primate live in large groups called troops.

Lemur species vary a lot. Some are active during the day, while others are up and about at night. Some like to live on their own, while other species prefer to live in groups. Nearly all are threatened or **endangered** in the wild.

Most lemurs move by leaping from tree to tree. They have strong back legs and long tails to help them balance.

# What are lemurs?

Lemurs are **prosimians**, which means "before apes". They are less closely related to humans than monkeys and apes are, and are closer to early primates of millions of years ago.

## Where do lemurs live?

Lemurs can be found in the wild only in Madagascar, off the south-eastern coast of Africa, and the nearby Comoros Islands. Lemurs have lived there for 50 million years. It is thought that they may have floated across to the island on vegetation.

Lemurs live in Madagascar. Close relatives of lemurs include pottos, bush babies, and lorises.

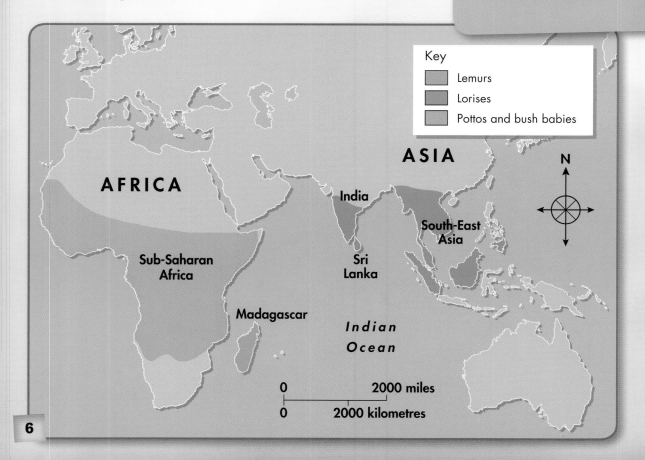

Key
- Lemurs
- Lorises
- Pottos and bush babies

ASIA

AFRICA

India

South-East Asia

Sub-Saharan Africa

Sri Lanka

Madagascar

*Indian Ocean*

N

0          2000 miles
0      2000 kilometres

Most prosimians in Africa were eventually replaced by monkeys. Monkeys did not make it across to Madagascar, however. This lack of competition allowed lemurs to flourish there. Less than 2,000 years ago humans arrived in Madagascar. Since then, lemurs have gradually been forced out of their natural **habitats** and a number of **species**, including the giant sloth lemur, have died out.

## Lemur features

Lemurs have soft fur and long, furry tails. Prosimians have a toilet claw on their second toe and dental or tooth combs which are used for grooming. Lemurs have eyes at the front of their heads, which gives them a wide view and allows them to judge distances well. A light-reflecting layer in the eye helps them to see at night.

Ring-tailed lemurs can live for up to 18 years in the wild.

## Smell

Lemurs have pointed snouts, and their sense of smell is much stronger than their sense of sight. This is the opposite of monkeys and other primates. The sense of smell is important for finding food. Lemurs also have powerful scent glands which they use to mark **territory.** Females use scent to show they are ready to mate, and males use it to attract females.

# How are lemurs classified?

**Classifying** things is the way that humans try to make sense of the living world. Grouping living things together by the characteristics that they share allows us to identify them and understand why they live where they do and behave as they do.

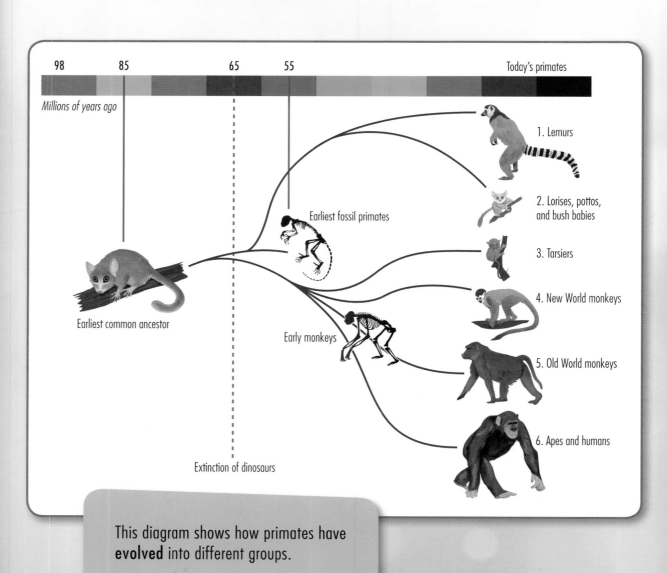

98    85              65        55                                    Today's primates

*Millions of years ago*

Earliest fossil primates

1. Lemurs

2. Lorises, pottos, and bush babies

3. Tarsiers

4. New World monkeys

Earliest common ancestor

Early monkeys

5. Old World monkeys

6. Apes and humans

Extinction of dinosaurs

This diagram shows how primates have **evolved** into different groups.

## Classification groups

In classification, animals are split into various groups. The standard groups are kingdom, phylum, class, order, family, genus, and **species**. Sometimes, further classification involves adding more groups such as a suborder or infraorder. Each of the standard groups contains fewer and fewer members. For example, there are far more animals to be found in the class Mammalia (**mammals**) than in the family Lemuridae (lemurs). Animals are given an internationally recognized two-part Latin name. This helps to avoid confusion if animals are known by different common names in different countries. For example, the ring-tailed lemur has the Latin name *Lemur catta*.

## Strepsirrhini

Strepsirrhini (**prosimians**) is a suborder of primates. The suborder includes lemurs, bush babies, pottos, and lorises. There are five families of lemurs. The true lemurs include ring-tailed lemurs, ruffed lemurs, and brown lemurs. Sportive lemurs include the Northern sportive lemur and Milne-Edwards' sportive lemur. Woolly lemurs, sifakas, and indris make up another family. Dwarf and mouse lemurs are grouped together with fork-crowned lemurs, and the aye-aye is in a family of its own.

### BLACK LEMURS – OR ARE THEY?

Male and female black lemurs were originally thought to be different species because they look so different. Males are black but females are reddish-brown and have light-coloured bellies and ear tufts.

## Controversy

It is thought that there are about 100 known living species of lemur, which is an increase on the 50 thought to be in existence in 1994. This increase is mainly because of the **conservation** focus on Madagascar in recent years, during which many more lemur species have been discovered. Scientists do not all agree on this issue, however. Some experts think that new species are announced too quickly without investigating properly to check that they are new species. This is perhaps done in order to increase the pressure on the government to put in place more protection for the lemurs' **habitats**.

## Tarsiers

Tarsiers are another type of primate that was at one stage included with prosimians. However, they are now placed in a different suborder, linked with monkeys and apes. They look similar to bush babies but their sight is much better than that of other prosimians, and they make less use of smell.

## CHARLIE WELCH AND ANDREA KATZ

Scientists Charlie Welch and Andrea Katz were involved in the Madagascar Fauna Group. This was set up in 1988 after the government of Madagascar asked for help with conservation. It is an international group of zoos and other institutions that work together to help save Madagascar's animals and habitats. Welch and Katz helped to set up a captive breeding programme that allowed lemurs to be **reintroduced** into the wild for the first time in 1997. Welch and Katz worked in Madagascar for 17 years.

The mongoose lemur is about the size of a cat. It eats fruit, nectar, and the flowers of the kapok tree.

Kingdom: Animalia

Phylum: Chordata

Subphylum: Vertebrata

Class: Mammalia

Order: Primates

Suborder: Strepsirrhini

Family: Lemuridae

Genus: Eulemur

Species: Eulemur mongoz

This diagram shows how the mongoose lemur is classified.

# Where do lemurs live?

A **habitat** is the place where an animal lives. The habitat has to provide everything the animal needs from food and water to shelter.

## Lemur habitats

Lemurs live in a range of habitats, including **rainforests**, dry forests, scrubland, and dry spiny forests. They prefer primary forests – those that are untouched by humans. Unfortunately, there are not many left.

Ruffed lemurs live in rainforests in eastern Madagascar. Rainforests are very hot and wet all year round, so very tall trees grow there. Sportive lemurs live in all areas of Madagascar, including dry forests with their tall trees and bamboo plants. Mongoose lemurs on the Comoros Islands tend to inhabit humid forests, while those on Madagascar live on dry forested coastal land. Dwarf lemurs can be found mainly in lowland rainforests. The aye-aye seems to be able to live in many different habitats, including rainforest and deciduous forest (forest containing trees that lose their leaves every year).

Rainforests are home to large numbers of animals and plants.

## Sifakas and indris

Diademed sifakas live in rainforests. Some Verreaux's sifakas live in scrubland in southern Madagascar, where there are many huge spiny cactus-like plants. Sifakas leap from one plant to another without landing on the spines. Indris live in mountain forests in north-eastern Madagascar.

## Other prosimians

Bush babies often live in tree hollows in east Africa or in woodlands and bushlands in sub-Saharan Africa. Slow lorises live in south-east Asia in **tropical** rainforests. Slender lorises live in tropical forests in India and Sri Lanka. Pottos mainly live in tropical rainforests in western Africa. They make their homes in trees that are up to 30 metres (98 feet) tall. They can also be found in coastal forests.

The world's largest lemur is the indri. It spends nearly all its time in trees.

# What adaptations help lemurs survive?

An **adaptation** is something that allows an animal to live in a particular place in a particular way. Animals develop adaptations as **species evolve** over thousands of years.

## Vision

Lemurs have forward-facing eyes so they are able to judge distances well, which is useful for leaping from tree to tree. Many species do not have colour vision because they are nocturnal, and being able to see colour is not useful in the dark. Instead they have a layer of cells, called the *tapetum lucidum*, behind the retinas of their eyes. This helps them to see better in the dark by reflecting light back through the retina. Many nocturnal animals have this adaptation.

The *tapetum lucidum* is the reason why lemurs' eyes shine brightly if a light is shone at them or if a photograph is taken in dim light.

## Scent

Lemurs have long moist noses because smell is more important to them than it is to other primates. Scent is used for **territory** marking, finding food, and breeding. Different species have scent glands in different places. The male ring-tailed lemur has a scent gland on its forearms, while the woolly lemur has glands in its neck. Other species have scent glands on their feet or rears.

## The aye-aye

The aye-aye has big ears to help it hear grubs moving around in trees. It also has a long finger with a claw that it uses to pull grubs out of the tree trunk. The aye-aye uses its strong teeth, which never stop growing, to gnaw a hole in the bark of the tree.

The aye-aye uses its long finger to tap a tree and then listen for grubs moving around.

## Grooming

The tooth comb is a group of six teeth sticking straight out from a lemur's jaw. Lemurs use it to groom themselves or other lemurs. **Prosimians** also have a toilet claw, which is a long, thin claw on the second toe. This is useful for grooming. Apart from the toilet claw, they have soft hands with fingers. These fingers have flat nails, similar to human fingers. Many prosimians also have **opposable thumbs** for gripping branches.

### AN EXTRA TONGUE!

Bush babies have two tongues! They have a tooth comb just like other prosimians. The second tongue is specially adapted for cleaning the tooth comb! It has **denticles** that fit between the grooves of the tooth comb to remove hairs after grooming.

These crowned lemurs are grooming each other.

## Movement

Sifakas tend to stay upright as they leap to and from *Didierea* plants. However, if the plants are too far apart, sifakas can come down to the ground and use their strong back legs to cross the distance in between the plants. They travel by hopping sideways on their feet, with their arms out for balance. Bush babies also jump from tree to tree so they have long back legs and a bushy tail. A lemur's long tail is used for balance. The indri is the only lemur species with a short tail.

Sifakas look as if they are dancing as they move across the ground.

# What do lemurs eat?

Animals eat other animals or plants and, in turn, may be eaten by other animals. These links between animals and plants are called food chains. Many connected food chains add up to a food web. The more connections in a food web, the less affected it would be if one member of it died out.

In the diagram below, the number of lemurs is affected by the amount of fruit and leaves available for them to eat. If the forests are destroyed, less food will be available and the lemur may die out. This would also affect fossas, whose main food is lemurs.

This food web includes two different kinds of lemurs that eat the same type of food.

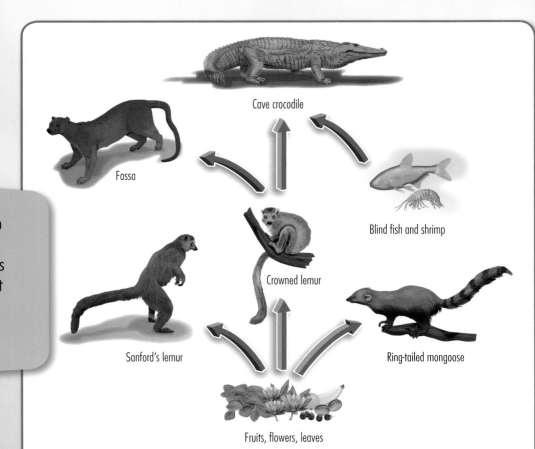

Cave crocodile

Fossa

Blind fish and shrimp

Crowned lemur

Sanford's lemur

Ring-tailed mongoose

Fruits, flowers, leaves

## Predators and prey

A food chain starts with a plant because plants can make their own food. They are called producers. Animals are called consumers because they consume (eat) other animals or plants.

Animals such as lemurs are called omnivores because they eat fruit and leaves but also sometimes eat small animals or eggs. Animals that eat lemurs include fossas, crocodiles, hawks, and snakes. These animals are carnivores (meat-eaters). Animals that eat other animals are known as predators. The animals they eat are known as prey.

## Not all the same

Ring-tailed lemurs are a bit different from other lemurs. They are known as "opportunistic omnivores". This means that although they normally eat plants and fruit, if these foods are not available they will eat insects and small animals.

## Eating soil

Lemurs also eat soil. This may seem strange but there are several possible reasons for it. It is thought that it may help lemurs by adding certain **nutrients** to their diet that they do not get from their normal food. They might also eat soil to help soak up plant poisons.

Most lemurs eat fruit and leaves.

19

# What is a lemur's life cycle?

The life cycle of an animal covers its birth to its death and all the different stages in between.

## Mating

Different **species** of lemur behave differently when it comes to choosing a partner. Most lemurs have several partners. In some groups, a couple of breeding females mate with a single male. An indri chooses one partner to mate with and they stay together until one of them dies.

The mating season is very short for most lemurs. Female lemurs may have only a few days of the year during which they can become pregnant. Mating happens towards the end of the dry season so that the babies are born in the wet season. This is because there is more food available in the wet season. If there is a lack of food, lemurs will not mate.

## Pregnancy and birth

A lemur pregnancy usually lasts for about two to five months. They often give birth in a tree hollow or a nest. Usually only one baby is born at a time but some lemurs may have twins. Bush babies can also have triplets, while ruffed lemurs can have up to six babies in one go.

### GHOSTS

Lemurs are named after ancient Roman *lemures* (ghost-like figures). It is thought that this is because of lemurs' shiny eyes and ghostly howling. In ancient Rome, dead spirits were said to stare at the living with great shining eyes.

Lemur babies cling on to their mothers' fur. For the first few weeks they cling underneath their mothers, then they ride on their mothers' backs.

## SINGING FOR LOVE

Some species of mouse lemur look so similar it can be difficult to tell them apart in the dark. As mouse lemurs are nocturnal this can cause problems when it comes to mating! Males use calls to advertise that they want to mate. Researchers played the calls of three species to a grey mouse lemur and watched her reactions. She responded most to the grey mouse lemur call. The calls help mouse lemurs to avoid wasting time mating with the wrong species.

## Young lemurs

Babies are born covered in fur and with their eyes open. They are helpless when first born and are carried in their mothers' mouths. The mother feeds the baby with her milk for a few weeks. Most lemurs are fully weaned by five months. This means they have learned to eat foods and do not rely on their mother's milk. They stay with their mothers for up to two years.

## The cycle begins again ...

The age at which a lemur can reproduce varies from species to species. The grey mouse lemur can have babies from about the age of one, while ring-tailed lemurs do not begin reproducing until the age of three. Lemurs may give birth every one or two years.

Once lemurs are able to have their own babies they start looking for a mate. Then the whole cycle begins again. Lemurs can live for up to 25 years in the wild and longer in captivity.

### EATING POISON

A golden bamboo lemur eats giant bamboo. This contains cyanide, a poison which can kill humans. The lemur has built up resistance to the poison, which means that the poison no longer affects it. It is thought to eat about 12 times more cyanide in a day than would kill other primates.

Playtime can involve all kinds of fun, including swinging on a tree branch!

# How do lemurs behave?

Behaviour can vary a lot among lemur **species** but there are some things that they have in common.

## Smell-orientated communication

Male ring-tailed lemurs try to outstink each other in mating season! They wipe scent from their wrists on to the ends of their tails and then wave them about to spread the smell. The female decides which one she prefers. This behaviour can also be used to warn off other groups. Other **prosimians** such as bush babies mark their **territory** with scent. Before they leave their shelters they spray urine on to their hands and feet. As they move through the trees, they leave behind their smell.

Bush babies really do have smelly feet!

## Vocal communication

Lemurs tend to be very vocal. Red-ruffed lemurs have about twelve different calls to warn of predators. Indris sing to mark their territory – often for several minutes at a time – and they can be heard over 1.5 kilometres (0.9 miles) away. Sometimes lemurs call to tell other members of their group where they are.

## Body language

Ring-tailed lemurs keep their tails up in the air while on the move, so that the whole group can keep track of each other. Their tails are used like flags. Facial expressions are also used in ring-tailed lemur groups. For example, staring with the corners of the mouth pulled back to barely show the teeth shows friendliness. However, facial expressions are used a lot less by lemurs than by monkeys. This is because the nose of a lemur is connected to its upper lip and gum. This limits the expressions lemurs can make.

Lemurs mark trees with their scent to warn other groups to keep out of their territory.

## Female leaders

Females are leaders in most lemur groups. Female ring-tailed lemurs stay with the group into which they were born. Males roam from group to group. Ring-tailed lemur females show aggressive behaviour towards males, for example lunging, chasing, and biting. Males tend to be submissive, which means they usually do as they are told! However, crowned lemur males are only submissive when the females are aggressive towards them. Female indris always feed first. The males have to wait. If they get impatient and try to join the females, they get cuffed!

## HANTA RASAMIMANANA

Hanta Rasamimanana is known as Madagascar's "lemur lady" because she has worked hard to try to save lemurs from **extinction**. In the 1980s she was sent by the Malagasy government to report on what Alison Jolly, a primatologist who was studying lemurs at the time, was doing. Rasamimanana soon forgot about spying and fell in love with the lemurs! She now teaches children about lemurs and the difficulties they face in the wild.

## Sunbathing

One of the best known lemur behaviours involves something many humans like doing too – sunbathing! After a cold night, some lemurs like nothing more than lying on a rock with arms and legs spread out, warming themselves in the sun. Sifakas have thin sections of skin called membranes in between their arms and chest, which help to absorb the heat quickly. Sunbathing is often a social occasion for ring-tailed lemurs and sifakas. They allow their bodies to warm up and then go looking for food.

According to some people in Madagascar, sifakas are thought to worship the sun because they like to sunbathe first thing in the morning.

## Grooming

Grooming is useful because it helps to get rid of ticks and fleas but it is also social, allowing lemurs to maintain relationships. They use their tooth combs on themselves and on others. Ring-tailed lemurs sometimes give purrs of contentment during grooming sessions.

## Caring for young

Ring-tailed lemurs care for their young differently from other species. The babies are looked after and even fed by females other than the mother. This means that the mother can have time to rest or more time to find food. Also, young females can gain practice caring for infants. Babies can also be adopted by another female if the mother dies. Sometimes weasel sportive lemur babies and potto babies are left on a branch, hidden from predators, while the mother goes off to search for food.

### CHANGE OF HABIT

Most true lemurs are cathemeral, which means they are active in bursts in the day and at night. The mongoose lemur is a bit different – it is nocturnal during the dry season but diurnal (active during the day) in the wet season. This is because it gets extremely hot in the daytime during the dry season. The mongoose lemur very sensibly waits for the cooler evening before searching for food.

## Time for a nap

In the dry season, when food is scarce, most mouse lemurs are inactive for several days. They store fat in their tails and hind legs to help get them through this period. Dwarf lemurs **hibernate** for at least five months, and are the only primates known to do so. They also have long tails that can store fat.

Dwarf lemurs are nocturnal and live in almost all **habitats** in Madagascar.

# A DAY IN THE LIFE OF A LEMUR

Many lemurs are nocturnal (active at night) but the ring-tailed lemur is diurnal (active during the day). Ring-tailed lemurs live in forests in south-west Madagascar. Each troop is led by females and has its own territory. Scent-marking and vocal communication are used to let other groups know boundaries.

Ring-tailed lemurs live in groups of up to 30.

## THE MORNING

Ring-tailed lemurs spend about a third of their day on the ground but they sleep in trees. Before dawn, they awaken and spend some time moving around in the trees. In the early morning, they climb down to sit in the sun. With legs spread and arms resting on their knees, they soak up the sun's warmth. Ring-tailed lemurs live in areas that can get very cold at night so they need to warm up before **foraging** for food.

## FEEDING

Lemurs forage for food till noon, when they find shade and have a rest. More foraging takes place in the early afternoon, with another rest period if it is hot. In the driest areas, ring-tailed lemurs sometimes have to pay daily visits to underground rivers for drinking water. They can also get water from plants such as aloe.

You can see this lemur's tooth comb right at the front of its lower jaw.

## NIGHT-TIME

In the late afternoon, the lemurs return to the trees. They may still move around and groom each other before huddling together and going to sleep.

# How intelligent are lemurs?

**Prosimians** are usually thought of as the least intelligent of the primates but there have been very few studies carried out compared to those done on monkeys and apes. They could be more intelligent than we think!

Blue-eyed lemurs are the only primates apart from humans to have blue eyes.

## Safe food

The vomeronasal organ, on the roof of a lemur's mouth, is a special sensory organ that lemurs have developed. It helps lemurs select non-poisonous leaves to eat. Sometimes, though, the chemical structure of a plant can change and it can become poisonous. Lemurs use a "tester" to find out if the food is safe to eat. The tester is always a healthy adult who gradually increases their intake of the food each day. If they survive after three days, only then will the rest of the group eat the particular food.

## Group work

Some lemurs **forage** for food in groups, which allows them to cover a wider area. It also means that there are more eyes and ears watching for predators. Even lemurs that forage alone usually sleep in groups. They settle on slender branches so that they can feel the vibration if a predator gets close. The vibrations act as a warning system.

## INTELLIGENCE TESTS

Lemurs recently surprised researchers during intelligence tests carried out in the United States. The lemurs learned to press their noses against a computer screen to correctly order long lists of pictures that they had memorized. It is possible that in previous intelligence tests researchers tried to get lemurs to use their hands, as monkeys do. It could be that lemurs are just not as skilled with their hands rather than not being as clever as other primates.

Feeding together means that these brown lemurs can feel safer from predators.

It is thought that 50 per cent of the world's primates are in danger of **extinction** in the near future. This is due to a number of reasons, all of which are linked to humans.

## NOT REALLY EXTINCT

Sibree's dwarf lemur was first seen in 1896. Not seen at all during the 20th century, it was thought to be **extinct**. However, in 2001 researchers found a dwarf lemur that was confirmed in 2010 as a Sibree's dwarf lemur. People now have the chance to try to protect the **species**.

## Habitat loss

The human population is expanding all the time. As more humans are born, more land is needed for food production and for housing. Humans are taking over the natural **habitats** of not just lemurs but other animals and birds, too. It is a particular issue for Madagascar because the country is so poor.

Two-thirds of the population, or about 13 million people, earn less than US$1 a day. Many people from Madagascar rely on the land much more than people in more developed countries. Many wild habitats are being lost through clearing land for planting rice.

Since humans first arrived in Madagascar less than 2,000 years ago, 80 per cent of forest cover has been lost. This has mainly been due to clearing land for farming and cutting down trees for fuel and furniture. Deforestation is a major threat because so many lemurs live in trees.

Local people use slash-and-burn farming methods. This involves cutting down trees and bushes, allowing the land to dry, and then setting fire to it. This clears the land for planting crops.

## Climate change

Lemurs are affected by climate change. When it rains heavily, lemurs do not search for food – they wait for the rain to stop. Fruit may also be knocked from the trees by heavy rain, making it more difficult for mothers to feed their babies. Infants who are not fed properly cannot survive.

## Political problems

Political problems in Madagascar are a threat to lemurs. Unstable government can lead to less habitat protection. For example, after a government takeover in 2009, loggers were soon busy clearing land that was supposed to be protected. Some people involved in **conservation** were threatened, forcing them to leave the country. The previous government had supported conservation attempts, but the new one seemed less concerned. Backward steps like this will only cause further harm to the animals living in Madagascar.

Lorises are sometimes sold as pets. They have been found kept in extremely small cages.

# Hunting

Bushmeat is the term used for meat that comes from wild animals, including lemurs. Bushmeat is a problem despite the fact that the killing of lemurs or selling them as pets has been illegal since 1964. In some areas, dogs are used for hunting ring-tailed lemurs. In others, Verreaux's sifaka is known by local people as *sifaka-bilany* or "sifaka of the cooking pot". Many people often rely on bushmeat to survive – they need the money they get from selling it as well as the food for themselves. This makes it a difficult issue to deal with.

This family is one of the many that needs to sell bushmeat in order to survive.

# Other threats

Being captured to be sold as pets is another threat that lemurs face. In some areas, lemurs are considered bad luck, so are killed on sight by local people.

# How can people help lemurs?

Primates, including lemurs, are close relatives of humans, yet humans have brought them close to **extinction**. We need to protect lemurs and **conserve** their **habitats**, partly because we can learn about primate development from them.

A researcher is studying lemurs in order to be better able to help them.

## Conservation organizations

**Conservation** organizations help not just by raising money but also in practical ways. Conservationists encourage local people to want to protect their local wildlife and their habitats. Beza Mahafaly Special Reserve is a research and training centre for students and local people in south-west Madagascar. They run courses to teach local people about different methods of growing food, for example.

## Eco-tourism

**Eco-tourism** can be used to help lemurs by providing an alternative source of income for local people. Many tourists are interested in seeing animals in the wild, but often need a guide to show them where to go and how to behave with the animals. Local people can do this job and other jobs linked to tourism.

## What can you do

- You can join conservation groups, such as the World Wildlife Fund (WWF) and Conservation International, and perhaps donate some pocket money every now and then.

- Encourage your family not to buy furniture made from the wood of **rainforest** trees.

- If you go shopping for food with your parents, you can ask them to buy goods that have been produced in an environmentally friendly way. Food labels will give information on this. Fairtrade goods ensure that money is earned by local people, which may mean they do not have to take part in activities that may harm lemurs.

- Read about lemurs and tell your friends and family about what you find out. The more people who know about **endangered** lemurs, the better.

- Finally, make sure you recycle as much as possible. This means that materials such as wood can be saved and reused rather than more trees being cut down.

# What does the future hold for lemurs?

Lemurs face many threats, and some **species** are likely to become **extinct** in the near future. At the moment, the species **extinction** rate across all animals is 1,000 to 10,000 times higher than it would be naturally – without humans.

On the positive side, however, **conservation** groups are working hard to make sure that lemur species are as protected as possible. Conservation programmes such as Save Our Species (SOS) set up by the International Union for Conservation of Nature (IUCN) are important in showing the world the danger some animals are in. Madagascar is also one of the top priorities for international conservation because there are so many species living there that do not live anywhere else.

Lemurs come in all shapes and sizes! This mouse lemur is the tiniest lemur of all.

## Local people

Working with local people and encouraging them to feel pride in these wonderful animals is also vital to conservation. One conservation project involved experts from Bangor University in Wales and people from Madagascar getting together. They shared knowledge and skills to try to prevent lemurs being caught for bushmeat.

## Reintroduction to the wild

Recently, the idea of **reintroducing** zoo animals to the wild has become more popular and has been relatively successful. The Madagascar Fauna Group was one of the first to try this. The Durrell Wildlife Conservation Trust has a captive breeding programme, and is involved in conservation and research. Captive breeding means animals are raised in zoos then reintroduced into their natural habitat.

It is important that we do not allow lemurs to die out. They deserve their place in the natural world. The more young people – like you! – who get involved, the better.

Lemurs tend to have only one baby at a time so if disaster occurs their population cannot recover as quickly as other creatures.

# Lemur profiles

red fur

Ruff under chin and around cheeks

moist nostrils

pointed snout

**Species:** red-ruffed lemur

**Weight:** 3–4.5 kilograms (6½–10 pounds)

**Height [not including tail]:** 110–120 centimetres (43–47 inches)

**Length of tail:** up to 65 centimetres (26 inches)

**Habitat:** dry forests

**Diet:** fruit, nectar, and pollen

**Number of young:** 2–6 infants born after 3–4 months of pregnancy. Females will give birth about once a year after they have reached maturity at 2 years of age.

**Life expectancy:** 15–20 years

neck spines, used for defence

short, woolly fur

pointed snout

flat nails

moist nostrils

**Species:** potto

**Weight:** 600–1,600 grams (1–3½ pounds)

**Height [not including tail]:** 30–39 centimetres (12–15 inches)

**Length of tail:** up to 10 centimetres (4 inches)

**Habitat:** forests and **tropical rainforests**

**Diet:** mainly fruit but occasionally slow-moving insects

**Number of young:** one infant born after 6–7 months of pregnancy. Females will give birth about once a year after they have reached maturity at 18 months.

**Life expectancy:** up to 26 years in captivity

# Glossary

**adaptation** body part or behaviour of a living thing that helps it survive in a particular habitat

**classify** group living things together by their similarities and differences

**conservation** protection or restoration of wildlife and the natural environment

**conserve** protect from harm or destruction

**denticle** small tooth-like part that sticks out

**eco-tourism** form of tourism that allows people to observe wildlife and help protect nature

**endangered** living thing that is at risk of dying out

**evolve** change gradually over time

**extinct** living thing that has died out

**extinction** when a living thing has died out

**forage** look for food over a wide area

**habitat** natural environment of a living thing

**hibernate** go into a long period of sleep, usually during the colder months

**mammal** animal that has fur or hair, gives birth to live young, and feeds its young on milk from the mother

**nutrient** substance that provides a living thing with the nourishment it needs to grow and live

**opposable thumb** thumb that can face and touch the fingers on the same hand

**prosimian** group of primates that includes lemurs, bush babies, lorises, and pottos

**rainforest** forest with tall, thickly-growing trees in an area with high rainfall

**reintroduce** put a living thing back into its natural environment

**species** group of similar living things that can mate with each other

**territory** area of land that an animal claims as its own

**tropical** regions of Earth around the equator

# Find out more

## Books

*100 Things You Should Know About Monkeys and Apes*, Camilla de la Bedoyere (Miles Kelly, 2008)

*Classifying Living Things: Classifying Mammals*, Andrew Solway (Raintree, 2009)

*Protecting Food Chains: Rainforest Food Chains*, Heidi Moore (Raintree, 2010)

## Websites

**www.bristolzoo.org.uk/mammals**
This site has lots of information about mammals, including lemurs.

**www.bbc.co.uk/nature/life/Primate**
Learn about lemurs and other primates on this BBC website.

## Organizations to contact

**World Wildlife Fund UK**
**www.wwf.org.uk**
WWF works to protect animals and nature, and needs your help! Have a look at their website and see what you can do.

**Endangered Species International**
**www.endangeredspeciesinternational.org/index.php**
This organization focuses on saving endangered animals around the world.

**Durrell Wildlife Conservation Trust**
**www.durrell.org**
This organization aims to help save animal species from extinction.

# Index